ha•pa (hä'pä)
A Hawaiian word to describe a person of mixed-race heritage who identifies racially and culturally as both white and of Asian descent.

ISBN: 979-8-9879133-3-8

Text copyright © 2023 by Donna Le Virga
Illustrations copyright © 2023 by Ira Baykovska

All rights reserved. No part of this book may be reproduced or used in any manner without the prior written permission of the copyright owner, except for the use of brief quotations in a book review.

HAPPY HAPA
A YEAR OF TRADITIONS

By Donna Le Virga
Illustrated by Ira Baykovska

**Our sweet hapa. We are thrilled to be your parents.
Our world, our purpose is you.**

As parents with mixed backgrounds, we would like to take you on a tour of our family's history and traditions.

Meet your grandparents. They worked hard and made sacrifices to give us the home we have today. They traveled a long distance across great bodies of water.

One day, we will share with you just how far their journeys were.

Traditionally in our Chinese culture, 100 days after your birth marks an important milestone. We celebrate your 100th day by wishing you longevity and 100 years of life.

Grazie... Perfavore... Si... Ciao... Amore...

We embrace our unique cultures and speak multiple languages. We hope you enjoy learning about the vibrant customs that are important to us.

Happy Lunar New Year. We celebrate the beginning of a new year, a time to reunite with extended family, eat an abundance of Chinese dishes and pass out lucky red envelopes.

Buona Pasqua! During Easter holiday, we surround ourselves with loved ones as we share traditional meals and watch the children hunt for eggs.

While the weeks can get busy, our favorite time is when we can cook together and eat dinner as a family. We hope you find joy in cooking these delicious recipes with us.

to little Italy

We create memorable experiences by traveling to historic Italian neighborhoods. We explore and learn more about Italian food, history, and culture.

Qingming Festival is an annual Chinese holiday to honor our ancestors. We acknowledge those who have passed, but remain with us in spirit.

On Thanksgiving, we celebrate the harvest and bounty of the past year. We express gratitude for our health and daily blessings. Dad looks forward to the day you can catch a football.

The end of the year marks the festive season. We host a family gathering for the Feast of the Seven Fishes. Hopefully Santa delivers some nice presents under the Christmas tree.

Sweet hapa, we want to raise you to embrace the two worlds that are part of you. We acknowledge our traditions, all the while making new ones with you.

Acknowledgement

*To my son, Christian,
may you continue to embrace your heritage
for all the years to come.*

*Mama Le, you were the best of us.
Thank you for giving me your strength.*

About the Author

As a new mother of a hapa baby boy, Donna Le Virga discovered that there were hardly any multicultural children's books to fill her son's bookcase. This inspired her to write her own book, Happy Hapa, to read to her son. While earning a Bachelor of Arts degree in Economics and Chinese at the College of Holy Cross, she learned the importance of continuing Chinese studies in order to connect with her heritage. As Donna and her husband learn to navigate life as parents, they plan to pass down their Chinese- and Italian-American traditions to their son. They believe valuing these traditions will teach their son to appreciate and understand his identity as a hapa. Through this book, Donna hopes to keep her traditions alive and encourage readers of all backgrounds to do the same.

You can follow her on Instagram @deevirga

www.ingramcontent.com/pod-product-compliance
Lightning Source LLC
Chambersburg PA
CBHW040723060526
44119CB00083B/309